HYMNS
AND THEIR WRITERS.

BY

B. S. OLDING.

𝔄 paper read at Surbiton Park Lecture Hall.

LONDON:
ELLIOT STOCK, 62, PATERNOSTER ROW, E.C.
1899

PRICE FOURPENCE.

In the interest of creating a more extensive selection of rare historical book reprints, we have chosen to reproduce this title even though it may possibly have occasional imperfections such as missing and blurred pages, missing text, poor pictures, markings, dark backgrounds and other reproduction issues beyond our control. Because this work is culturally important, we have made it available as a part of our commitment to protecting, preserving and promoting the world's literature. Thank you for your understanding.

HYMNS AND THEIR WRITERS.

SHOULD this paper on this subject not prove an interesting one, I must accept all the demerit, for I am confident the subject itself is one which cannot fail to be deeply interesting to every religious man and woman.

How large a part do hymns occupy in the life of every one of us! How frequently do we find the best expression of our deepest sentiments in the language they supply! What tender associations are connected with their use in bygone times by dear friends who are no longer with us—recollections we would not willingly let die!

Even a moderate acquaintance with hymns will supply us with forms of words suited to all our varying moods. If our hearts are brimming over with thankfulness how, almost unconsciously, the words come into our minds:

'When all Thy mercies, O my God,
    My rising soul surveys,
Transported with the view, I'm lost
    In wonder, love, and praise!'

When oppressed by a sense of our own weakness and of the transitoriness of all things here, do not our hearts cry out:

'Our God, our help in ages past,
    Our hope for years to come,
Our shelter from the stormy blast,
    And our eternal home.'

When mourning the loss of loved ones removed by death, what consolation is brought to us by the words:

> 'Hear what the voice of God proclaims,
> For all the pious dead;
> Sweet is the savour of their names,
> And soft their sleeping bed.'

And when anticipating the inevitable close of our own earthly lives, and full of doubts as to what the next world may contain for us, cannot we say, and in saying it do we not realize peace and patience?—

> 'My knowledge of that life is small,
> The eye of faith is dim,
> Yet 'tis enough that Christ knows all,
> And I shall be with Him.'

There is another reason why hymns are of such great interest to us. We find in them the best illustration and proof of the existence of a true Catholic Church, embracing within its limits all followers of Christ.

Christian men are everywhere divided into sects. It must be so, and it is not to be regretted that it is so. Where the Spirit of God is there is liberty, and liberty to think freely must mean the existence of varying and opposite conclusions on almost every point. But, notwithstanding this, it is wholesome and refreshing to be able to find ground common to all Christian people, and I know of no other ground so truly common as this.

Take up any hymn-book you like, compiled of late years, and you will find, if you inquire into the authorship of the hymns, that every section of the Christian Church has supplied its quota; and it will not be until you have found the author's name that you will be able to determine whether the writer was a Roman Catholic or a Protestant, a Churchman or a Nonconformist, an Independent or a Baptist, a Presbyterian or a Unitarian.

You know the two hymns, the one beginning:

> 'In the cross of Christ I glory;
> Towering o'er the wrecks of time,
> All the light of sacred story
> Gathers round its head sublime;'

the other containing the verse:

> 'The cross! it takes our guilt away,
> It holds the fainting spirit up;
> It cheers with hope the gloomy day,
> And sweetens every bitter cup.'

It would be difficult from internal evidence to determine which was written by Bowring, the Unitarian, and which by Kelly, the Evangelical.

And here I may remark, in passing, that perhaps few of us may be aware that it is to the pen of a lady, who at the crisis of her religious life, when she was passing from orthodoxy to Unitarianism, we owe the hymn so deservedly popular among us:

> 'Nearer, my God, to Thee,
> Nearer to Thee!
> E'en though it be a cross
> That raiseth me.'

The fact is that hymns are not, except in some few instances, the embodiment of theological dogma or of ecclesiastical preference, but of something that lies much deeper and is of far greater value—the religious sentiment, found, as I believe, although in varying degree, in every human heart.

The best definition I can supply of a hymn would be—a rhythmical expression, more or less poetic, of religious emotion. You will notice the qualifying words 'more or less poetic.'

The poetic element should never be altogether absent, or the hymn will be commonplace, and may even descend to be mere doggerel; but I should be loath to exclude a composition from the category of good hymns because the poetry in it was not of the highest order. The best hymns are doubtless those containing the poetic element in high degree; but there are hymns, such as Watts'

> 'Come, we that love the Lord,
> And let our joys be known,'

which are little more than rhymed verses, which we should be sorry to part with, notwithstanding.

There are at least *four* qualities indispensable in the constitution of a *good* hymn.

1. Its language should be chaste and simple. There should be no straining after effect, no false or doubtful analogy, no exuberant hyperbole, no many-syllabled words. The more its language is as if from 'the well of English undefiled,' the more it resembles the simple diction of our Authorized Version, the higher it will rank.

2. It should embody a distinct idea or theme. It should not be diffuse, but should take one line of thought, and one only, so that we should receive the impression that its author was not a mere hymn-*maker*, but that he was for the time possessed with an idea which he desired to express and communicate. Its design should be apparent.

3. It should be complete in itself; that is to say, it should deal with its subject thoroughly and fully; it should have a natural beginning and a natural

ending; the thoughts pervading it should be consecutive.

4. It should express real and not affected sentiment. In other words, it should be sincere. It should not express the feelings we think we ought to possess, but those we actually possess. Of course it must not express such untruth as is to be found in Watts'

> 'Lord, what a wretched land is this,
>   That yields us no supply,
> No cheering fruits, no wholesome trees,
>   No streams of living joy;
> But pricking thorns thro' all the ground
>   And mortal poisons grow,
> And all the rivers that are found
>   With dangerous waters flow.'

Let us bear these tests in mind — put into one word, they are severally simplicity, expressiveness, completeness and sincerity—and apply them to our favourite hymns, and if they stand the test, we may congratulate ourselves upon the goodness of our judgment. If I were asked to name three hymns in which these qualities are most manifest, and which, therefore, I should regard as the best three in our language, I should select Newman's 'Lead, kindly Light,' Keble's 'Sun of my soul,' and Binney's 'Eternal Light'; but which I should put first I could not determine.

Look at 'Lead, kindly Light,' a little closely. As regards simplicity, it is almost entirely in monosyllables, comprehensible by a child, not commonplace but yet the language we use every day. Expressiveness: Its one idea of God's leading runs through every line. Completeness: It begins with the encircling gloom, the dark night; it ends:

'The night is gone,
And with the morn those angel faces smile,
Which I have loved long since, and lost awhile.'

Sincerity: If ever a hymn came from a man's heart, this did. Newman refers to the circumstances of his composing it in his 'Apologia.' He was ill at Palermo, aching to get home; he had a work to do in England. He was at the beginning of the long struggle of doubt as to where his duty lay, whether to remain in the Church of England or to abandon it for the Roman communion. He could not then determine what his future course should be. At no distant date he went over to the Church of Rome. I, for one, dare not say that in taking that step he was not following the leading of that 'kindly Light' whose help he craved so earnestly.

The same tests may be applied to 'Sun of my soul,' although I think its beauty and completeness are marred by the omission of the two verses with which the hymn really begins, and which give the keynote to the whole composition as an *evening* hymn. They are:

'' Tis gone, that bright and orbèd blaze,
Fast fading from our wistful gaze;
Yon mantling cloud has hid from sight
The last faint pulse of quivering light.

'In darkness and in weariness
The traveller on his way must press,
No gleam to watch on tree or tower,
Whiling away the lonesome hour.'

And then comes:

'Sun of my *soul*, Thou Saviour dear.'

Binney's hymn 'Eternal Light' is not so well known as it deserves to be, though it is sixty years and more since it was written. But for one verbal defect—the use of a double negative, which is clearly adopted only to eke out the metre in the second verse—it might be regarded as perfect. The third stanza, it is said, was often on the author's lips when near his own departure.

Hymns may be broadly divided into two categories—those for public and united use; those for private and individual use. It would be well if this distinction were always remembered. Unquestionably the hymns *most* suitable for public use are those which are distinctly hymns of worship, and more especially so in the case of Divine service amongst Nonconformists, when the people, not taking any (or if any, but small) part in audible prayer, should have ample opportunity of joining vocally in worship by means of the hymns chosen to be sung. They should be such that their language can be *sincerely* used by all present; such, for instance, as the beautiful hymn written by John Mason, a contemporary of Bunyan, and styled by Baxter 'the glory of the Church of England':

> 'Now from the altar of our hearts
> Let incense flames arise;
> Assist us, Lord, to offer up
> Our evening sacrifice.'

Milton's

> 'Let us with a gladsome mind
> Praise the Lord, for He is kind,'

is another model hymn for congregational use.

Let me name some few more hymns as illustrative of the type most appropriate for public use:

Hymns of adoration, praise, and thankfulness:

> 'All people that on earth do dwell,'

the authorship of which has never been determined, but is attributed to W. Kethe, of whom little is known.

'Before Jehovah's awful throne,'

written by Watts, the last stanza:

'Wide as the world is Thy command,
Vast as eternity Thy love,'

having been added by Charles Wesley.

Bowring's hymns:

'Father and Friend, Thy light, Thy love,
Beaming thro' all Thy works we see;'

and

'God is love, His mercy brightens
All the path in which we move.'

That glorious hymn of Watts'

'Jesus shall reign where'er the sun
Doth his successive journeys run.'

Hymns of confidence and trust. Doddridge's

'O God of Bethel, by whose hand
Thy people still are fed.'

Wesley's

'Thy ceaseless, unexhausted love,
Unmerited and free.'

Hymns of aspiration. Whittier's

'Dear Lord and Father of mankind,
Forgive our feverish ways.'

Bonar's

'When the weary, seeking rest,
To Thy goodness flee;
When the heavy-laden cast
All their load on Thee;'

and one of Page Hopps', which, as it is little known, I will quote in full:

'Father, let Thy kingdom come,
Let it come with living power;
Speak at length the final word,
Usher in the triumph hour.

'As it came in days of old,
   In the deepest hearts of men,
When Thy martyrs died for Thee,
   Let it come, O God, again.

'Tyrant thrones and idol shrines,
   Let them from their place be hurled;
Enter on Thy better reign,
   Wear the crown of this poor world.

'O what long, sad years have gone
   Since Thy Church was taught this prayer!
O what eyes have watched and wept
   For the dawning everywhere!

'Break, triumphant day of God!
   Break at last, our hearts to cheer;
Throbbing souls and holy songs
   Wait to hail Thy dawning here.

'Empires, temples, sceptres, thrones,
   May they all for God be won!
And in every human heart,
   Father, let Thy kingdom come.'

Though not strictly acts of worship, hymns of mutual encouragement may profitably be used, such as:

'Soldiers of Christ, arise.'
'Come, let us join our friends above.'
'Come, we that love the Lord.'

So also hymns anticipatory of a future life, so long as they are couched in modest language and do not pretend to a knowledge of that which none can know. Must we not put at the head of this list Watts'

'There is a land of pure delight'?

I must confess, however, that I am somewhat of a purist with respect to hymns suitable to be sung in public, and I would exclude almost entirely hymns in which the first person singular is used. They seem to me to contravene the fundamental idea of public worship, viz., that it should be *common* worship.

Neither would I admit those which purport to enforce some theological dogma, on the ground that such must inevitably tend to produce division rather than that brotherly union that common worship should promote. On the other hand, we should gladly welcome all hymns which have for their theme 'One is our Master, even Christ, and all we are brethren.'

Incomparably the best of this class is Whittier's 'Our Master,' from the stanzas of which two hymns suitable for public use have been formed, beginning respectively:

'Immortal love, for ever full,
  For ever flowing free,
For ever shared, for ever whole,
  A never-ebbing sea.'

'Our Friend, our Brother, and our Lord,
  What may Thy service be?
Nor name, nor form, nor ritual word,
  But simply following Thee.'

But let us now turn to hymns of a direct personal character, dealing with individual experience, and adapted for private use. The number suitable for public use is no doubt restricted, but here we have a practically unlimited supply. I shall only, however, refer to one great group, with which I am sure we have all of us more or less intimate acquaintance, for we have all had at times need of them. I mean hymns of consolation. These are so numerous it is difficult to make a selection, but amongst the very first that occur to me is Frances Power Cobbe's

'God draws a cloud over each gleaming morn:
    Would'st thou ask why?
It is because all noblest things are born
    In agony.

'Only upon *some* cross of pain or woe
        God's Son may lie:
Each soul redeemed from self and sin must know
        Its Calvary.

'Yet we must crave neither for joy nor grief:
        God chooses best;
He only knows our sick soul's best relief,
        And gives us rest.

'More than our feeble hearts can ever pine
        For holiness,
That Father in His tenderness divine
        Yearneth to bless.

'He never sends a joy not meant in love,
        Still less a pain;
Our gratitude the sunlight falls to prove;
        Our faith, the rain.

'In His hands we are safe. We falter on
        Through storm and mire;
Above, beside, around us, there is One
        Will never tire.

'What though we *fall*, and bruised and wounded, lie
        Our lips in dust!
God's arm shall lift us up to victory!
        In Him we trust.

'For neither life nor death, nor things below,
        Nor things above,
Can ever sever us, that we should go
        From His great love.'

Hardly less beautiful is Miss Winkworth's translation of Rodigast's hymn, beginning

        'Whate'er my God ordains is right,
            His will is ever just;
        Howe'er He orders now my cause,
            I will be still and trust.'

Another translation from the German by Whittier

is also deserving of remembrance. Its subject is 'Resignation,' and begins

> 'To weary hearts, to mourning homes,
> God's meekest angel gently comes.'

Nor must I omit to mention Vaughan's exquisite production, beginning

> 'They are all gone into the world of light,
> And I alone sit lingering here;
> Their very memory is fair and bright,
> And my sad thoughts doth cheer,'

and also containing the following exquisite verse:

> 'He that hath found some fledged bird's nest
> may know
> At first sight if the bird be flown;
> But what fair well or grove he sings in now,
> That is to him unknown.'

But for the fear that my paper would degenerate into a mere catalogue, I could mention many more of equal beauty. Suffice it to say, for any who may desire to find such hymns, that I know of no collection equal in fulness and richness to that made by the justly-venerated Dr. Martineau, entitled 'Hymns of Praise and Prayer.'

I cannot leave this subject without referring briefly to the hymns which no doubt many of us heard sung so exquisitely by the Jubilee Singers from America some years ago. They are well worth notice, notwithstanding their grotesqueness, because they are the natural expression of uncultured but deeply-religious natures. When we realize the conditions amidst which these songs came into existence—the cruel oppression involved in the state of slavery, the escape from which then seemed impossible—we shall appreciate the genuineness and the pathos of these productions. How natural that such words as these should arise from their lips:

'Nobody knows the trouble I see, Lord,
Nobody knows like Jesus.'

'Children, we shall all be free
When the Lord shall appear.'

'O Lord, O my good Lord,
Keep me from sinking down.'

'No more auction-block for me,
No more, no more.'

Cannot we imagine the comfort that crept into the souls of these poor people, and the strength and courage they gained by them? Truly, these were the work of the same Spirit which fills the greatest minds with the noblest thoughts.

Let us now turn from hymns to hymn-writers. What a wide field is opened to us here! It is difficult to determine the best method to proceed, but perhaps a rapid historical review of English writers will suit our purpose best. There was nothing worthy of the name of hymnody previous to the seventeenth century, although there was much of sacred poetry.

The first distinguished name we meet with is that of George Herbert, Rector of Bemerton, who may fitly be called the father of English hymnody. We are familiar with

'Teach me, my God and King,
In all things Thee to see,
And what I do in everything
To do it as for Thee.'

But there is another, not so well known, with this stirring stanza:

'Let all the world in every corner sing
  My God and King !
The heavens are not too high—
  His praise may thither fly ;
The earth is not too low—
  His praises there may grow.
Let all the world in every corner sing
  My God and King !'

Herbert was followed by Baxter, illustrious amongst the illustrious number of ejected clergymen of 1662. Imprisoned repeatedly, and through all his long life a sufferer from bodily weakness and pain, he was yet able to write :

'Lord, it belongs not to my care,
  Whether I die or live ;
To love and serve Thee is my share,
  And this Thy grace must give.

'If life be long, I will be glad
  That I may long obey ;
If short, yet why should I be sad,
  That shall have the same pay ?'

(Not 'To soar to endless day,' the allusion being to the parable of the labourers who received each a penny.)

'Christ leads me through no darker rooms
  Than He went through before ;
He that unto God's kingdom comes
  Must enter by this door.'

To the same age, but a little later, belongs Henry Vaughan, whose

'They are all gone into the world of light'

I have already quoted ; and Bishop Ken, the author of the famous morning and evening hymns :

'Awake, my soul, and with the sun
  Thy daily stage of duty run' ;

and

> 'Glory to Thee, my God, this night,'

or, as afterwards altered by himself,

> 'All praise to Thee, my God, this night.'

The only remaining writer of eminence of this period was Addison, whose five hymns—

> 'The Lord my pasture shall prepare,'
> 'When all Thy mercies, O my God,'
> 'The spacious firmament on high,'
> 'How are Thy servants blest, O Lord,'
> 'When rising from the bed of death'—

all appeared appended to articles in the *Spectator*, between July and October, 1712. The last but one,

> 'How are Thy servants,' etc.,

he describes as 'a Divine ode made by a gentleman upon the conclusion of his travels.' It was, in fact, written while sailing in the Mediterranean during a great storm, when the captain had given his vessel up for lost.

Up to this time hymns had been written almost exclusively for personal use, and not for public worship. A feeling existed against singing hymns as part of Christian worship, as strong as that which existed not long since in Scotland against the use of the organ, 'the kist of whistles,' as it was contemptuously called.

The Puritan objection to *forms* of prayer applied also to *forms* of praise, and not illogically, for the principle involved is the same in both cases. In some instances the desire to introduce hymn-singing led to rupture and secession, notably in the Baptist

16   Hymns and their Writers

Church under Benjamin Reach (its late pastor having been C. H. Spurgeon), where the majority were for hymn-singing, whereupon the minority betook themselves to a sanctuary where their consciences were not hurt by this new-fangled and dangerous innovation, as no doubt they regarded it. There were, however, some collections in existence, otherwise they would not have been fought over. It is probable—indeed, almost certain—that these contained few hymns of any merit, otherwise they would have survived to our days. Hymns had played up till this time no part in the religious life of the English nation. This will appear strange when we recall how in Germany both Huss and Luther awoke and promoted religious enthusiasm, and how largely the Reformation was helped by the use of their popular hymns. It is to be noted also that in the Churches founded by Calvin the same absence of hymns existed. The explanation of the non-use of hymns in England may lie in the fact that the theology of the English Puritans was much more Calvinistic than Lutheran, and it is notorious that the tendency of Calvinism has always been to discourage the introduction of any kind of art into Divine service. In any case, the English hymnody of the early part of the eighteenth century was both poor and scanty, and it is very interesting to know that this very poverty was the immediate *cause* of the great improvement that was about to take place.

It is related that young Isaac Watts, who we must regard as the founder of the modern hymnody, complained to his father of the character of the hymns sung at the Dissenting meeting at Southampton, where his father was deacon, whereupon his father bade him do what he could to mend the matter. He at once betook himself to composition, and produced the hymn

> 'Behold the glories of the Lamb
> Amidst His Father's throne!'

which stands first in his collection of hymns. This was followed by others, until there was enough to make a volume.

We are one and all familiar with Watts' hymns, many of us from our childhood. For myself, I think I may say I was brought up on Watts' hymns, nor do I regret it. But what must be our mature judgment on Watts as a hymnist? It has of late been the fashion to disparage him. But ought we to judge him by his best or by his worst? If the latter, the disparagement is justified; for he wrote some of the worst and most ridiculous hymns ever penned. It would be easy to quote illustrations of this, but for my own part I prefer to judge him by his best, and when I remember

> 'Awake our souls, away our fears,
> Let every trembling thought be gone;'
>
> 'I sing the Almighty power of God,
> That made the mountains rise;'
>
> 'Joy to the world, the Lord is come,
> Let earth receive her King;'
>
> 'Our God, our help in ages past,
> Our hope for years to come;'
>
> 'From all that dwell below the skies
> Let the Creator's praise arise;'
>
> 'Give me the wings of faith to rise
> Within the veil, and see;'
>
> 'The Lord my shepherd is—
> I shall be well supplied;'

and others I could name, but for wearying you, I conclude that he is entitled to a high place among hymn-writers, and that the Christian Church owes him an everlasting debt of gratitude.

His mistake was in writing too much, and he was evidently wanting in the critical faculty, or he certainly would not have written, or would subsequently have suppressed, at least four-fifths of his productions.

George Macdonald has truly said, 'How can any man write 600 religious poems and produce quality in proportion to quantity, save in an inverse ratio?'

Two writers must be mentioned before we come to a name as great as Watts—Robert Seagrave, author of

> 'Rise, my soul, and stretch thy wings,
> Thy better portion trace;'

and Philip Doddridge, also a Nonconformist minister. He was the author of 364 hymns, which circulated during his lifetime in MS. only. The following six will, I think, compare favourably with any six by any other single author:

> 'O God of Bethel, by whose hand.'
> 'Awake, my soul, stretch every nerve.'
> 'Hark the glad sound, the Saviour comes!'
> 'Ye servants of the Lord.'
> 'To-morrow, Lord, is Thine.'
> 'Great God, we sing that mighty Hand.'

His hymns were mostly composed to be read at the end of his sermons. How much more lasting the hymns have proved than the sermons!

And now of the Wesleys. Their hymns are so numerous as to fill thirteen volumes. Dr. Watts is regarded as voluminous because he wrote 600 hymns. What shall be said of Charles Wesley, who wrote more than as many thousands? Some are unquestionably of the highest order, but of many it must be said it had been better they had never been written.

This, however, was not the opinion of John Wesley, who in a preface to a collection of his brother's productions wrote: 'In these hymns there is no doggerel, no blotches, nothing put in to patch up the rhymes. Here are purity, strength, and plainness.' If the man to whom we owe the translation of the best German hymns was unable to see the defects so apparent to us, we wonder less at the marvellous popularity these hymns subsequently attained and still enjoy. Amongst Charles Wesley's best are the following well-known ones:

'Jesus, lover of my soul.'
'Soldiers of Christ, arise.'
'Thou hidden source of calm repose.'
'Leader of faithful souls and guide.'

Charles Wesley's hymns were original; John Wesley's were mostly translations from the Moravian, with which body he was in intimate relationship. Through him we thus have:

'Commit thou all thy griefs.'
'Lo, God is here! let us adore.'
'Thou hidden love of God, whose height.'

A little-known contemporary of the Wesleys, viz. Joseph Grigg, wrote two hymns well known to us—

'Jesus, and shall it ever be;'

and

'Behold a stranger at the door.'

I name them, not for any special excellence to be found in them, but for the interesting fact that they were written by a child, the former appearing in the *Gospel Magazine*, April, 1774, with the title 'Shame of Jesus conquered by Love; by a youth of ten years.' Many names of minor importance now meet us, the only conspicuous ones being Cowper and John Newton, whose histories were so intermingled, and to whose joint efforts the production of the 'Olney Hymns' are due. Cowper is the author of

'Hark, my soul, it is the Lord!'
'O for a closer walk with God!'
'God moves in a mysterious way'—

three hymns appreciated as much now as at any time.
Newton wrote

'How sweet the name of Jesus sounds.'
'Quiet, Lord, my froward mind.'

We lose sight of the narrowness of their theology in the breadth and depth of their religion.

Approaching more nearly to our own times, Thomas Kelly, an Irish clergyman, who died so recently as 1855, but of great age, was a voluminous writer of more than 700 hymns, some of them of great excellence and deservedly prized:

'We sing the praise of Him who died.'
'The head that once was crowned with thorns.'
'We've no abiding city here.'
'Look, ye saints! the sight is glorious.'

James Montgomery, Kelly's contemporary, wrote hymns we all know and admire:

'Hail to the Lord's anointed.'
'Millions within Thy courts have met.'
'O Spirit of the living God.'

Hymns and their Writers

But time fails me to recount the names of authors of beautiful hymns, now justly prized — many of them the writer of perhaps only one, but one we could not spare; for instance, Harriet Auber, who wrote 'Our blest Redeemer, ere He breathed'; John Marriott, 'Thou, whose Almighty word.' Of other writers, I can only mention Conder, Edmeston, Bowring, Keble, Lyte, Trench, Alford, Ellerton, Rawson, Gill, Blackie, Dix, and Monsell, whose fine hymn

'O worship the Lord in the beauty of holiness'

may fitly and frequently form part of our public worship.

One name I must specially mention, Samuel Greg; and I should much like, even at the risk of wearying you, to read a composition of his, than which I know none more expressive of the absolute trust and confidence in God we should desire to feel:

'Slowly, slowly darkening,
 The evening hours roll on;
And soon behind the cloud-land
 Will sink my setting sun.

'Around my path life's mysteries,
 Their deepening shadows throw;
And as I gaze and ponder,
 They dark and darker grow.

'But there's a Voice above me,
 Which says, "Wait, trust, and pray;
The night will soon be over,
 And light will come with day."

'Father! the light and darkness
 Are both alike to Thee;
Then to Thy waiting servant,
 Alike they both shall be.

'The great unending future,
 I cannot pierce its shroud;
Yet nothing doubt, nor tremble,
 God's bow is on the cloud.

'To Him I yield my spirit;
 On Him I lay my load:
Fear ends with death; beyond it
 I nothing see but God.

'Thus moving towards the darkness,
 I calmly wait His call,
Now seeing, fearing nothing;
 But hoping, trusting—all!'

Faber and Lynch, what different men! how opposite their theology, as well as their ecclesiastical convictions, and yet how alike in their hymns. The hymns of one are sometimes the counterparts of the other. Lynch sings:

'The Lord is rich and merciful.'

Faber:

'The heart of the Eternal is most wonderfully kind.'

Lynch:

'Where is thy God, my soul?
 Is He within thy heart?'

Faber:

'Deeper and deeper in my heart
 I feel Thee resting now.'

How strange that the words

'There's a wideness in God's mercy
Like the wideness of the sea.
There's a kindness in His justice
Which is more than liberty,
For the love of God is broader
Than the measures of man's mind,
And the heart of the Eternal
Is most wonderfully kind'

should have been written by a devoted adherent of that Church which maintains that there is no certainty of salvation outside its pale.

Lynch's collection, called 'The Rivulet,' for which he was forty years since deemed a heretic, is a prized possession of all hymn-lovers who once become acquainted with it. Many of his hymns are now well known, such as

> 'Gracious Spirit, dwell with me.'
> 'Dismiss me not Thy service, Lord.'
> 'Say not, my soul, "From whence
>   Can God relieve my case?"'
> 'Mountains by the darkness hidden,'

and as greatly valued.

I must read a beautiful one, very little known:

> 'The world was dark with care and woe,
>   With brawl and pleasure wild,
> When in the midst, His love to show,
>   God set a Child.
>
> 'The sages frowned, their beards they shook,
>   For pride their heart beguiled;
> They said, each looking on his book:
>   "We want no child."
>
> 'The merchants turned towards their scales,
>   Around their wealth lay piled;
> Said they: "'Tis gold alone prevails:
>   We want no child."
>
> 'The soldiers rose in noisy sport,
>   Disdainfully they smiled,
> And said: "Can babes the shield support?
>   We want no child."
>
> 'The merry sinners laughed or blushed;
>   Alas! and some reviled;
> All cried, as to the dance they rushed:
>   "We want no child."

> 'The old, the afflicted, and the poor,
>   With voices harsh or mild,
> Said: "Hope to us returns no more;
>   We want no child."
>
> 'And men of grave and moral word,
>   With consciences defiled,
> Said: "Let the old truth still be heard;
>   We want no child."
>
> 'Then said the Lord, "O world of care,
>   So blinded and beguiled,
> Thou must become for thy repair,
>   A holy child.
>
> '"And unto thee a Son is born,
>   Thy second hope has smiled;
> Thou mayst, though sin- and trouble-worn,
>   Be made a child."'

Of female writers, can anything be said too good of Charlotte Elliott, Adelaide Procter, Frances Havergal, Anna Waring, and Sarah Adams, who have all passed away, but who will, one and all, be long remembered with gratitude by many hearts which have gained comfort and strength and hope through their unequalled productions.

Hymns perfectly suitable for children are, unhappily, very few, notwithstanding the fact that there has been great improvement in them.

Children were once required to commit to memory words that conveyed to them false ideas of God, and that tended to crush out of their young hearts all yearning after their loving Father, and that became a heavy burden for many long years. I can speak from my own experience, and can vividly recall the terror inspired by Watts' hymn beginning 'There is a dreadful hell.' Thank God children no longer have such burdens laid on them! But is there not

Hymns and their Writers 25

still much unreality and sentimentality in the hymns now in use by children?

How utterly unreal, and therefore harmful, for a child to be taught to say, 'I want to be an angel'! And does not this remark apply equally to all hymns about heaven: 'There is a happy land,' and others of that kind? Those who have borne some of the heat and burden of the day may naturally and fitly comfort themselves with thoughts of a better life beyond; but it is mere affectation in the mouths of children to express dissatisfaction with the present world and a longing for a better. Children are quick to perceive this unreality, and it insensibly gives an air of unreality to all the religious teaching they receive.

All children should be taught to commit hymns to memory; but what hymns? The question is a very difficult one, and I have sometimes thought, and am still inclined to think, that this is the right conclusion: that the best hymns for children are those that are the best for adults, and not so-called children's hymns at all.

The best hymns for adults are those in which trust in God, love of God, desire to please Him, charity to our fellows, are expressed in simplest language, and so expressed, are to be laid hold of by children just as much as by others. There may possibly be occasionally phrases and allusions in such hymns beyond children's comprehension, but these will be easily capable of explanation. The appeal to their imagination may even assist to fix the hymns in remembrance. Such hymns, and a very small number of carefully selected ones especially intended for children, will prove of an inestimable service, both in childhood and in later life. The best, because the simplest and truest, hymn for children that I have met with is the following:

> 'My Father, hear my prayer
>   Before I go to rest;
> It is Thy little child
>   That cometh to be blest.
>
> 'Forgive me all my sin,
>   And let me sleep this night
> In safety and in peace
>   Until the morning light.
>
> 'Lord, help me every day
>   To love Thee more and more,
> And try to do Thy will
>   Much better than before.
>
> 'Now look upon me, Lord,
>   Ere I lie down to rest;
> It is Thy little child
>   That cometh to be blest.'

Let me say finally upon this subject that, if it is well we should submit the hymns we use ourselves to a wise criticism, the obligation to do the same for children's hymns is tenfold stronger.

And now let me say a few words before concluding on a subject on which I hold a very strong opinion indeed. I refer to the permissibility of alterations in and additions to hymns as they come from their authors.

I do not mean such trifling matters as the substitution of a modern word for one that has gone out of use and has become grotesque—such, for instance, as

> 'His heart is made of tenderness,
> His bowels melt with love.'

Well, you know it was at one time thought that the bowels were the seat of the affections. We read: 'Joseph's bowels did yearn upon his brother.' That is a figure of speech that in a hymn would be too ludicrous for us to sing; an alteration in such case is not only permissible, but desirable. I am speaking of much more serious matters—cases, for instance, in which the theological views of some people are not expressed by the author, and when a verse embodying those views is added. A case in point,

'Nearer, my God, to Thee,'

in the Baptist hymn-book, has the following stanza:

'Christ alone beareth me
  Where Thou dost shine;
Joint heir He maketh me
  Of the Divine.
In Christ my soul shall be,
Nearer, my God, to Thee,' etc.

Such an addition is, in my opinion, utterly unwarrantable.

In the old Congregational Hymn-Book the stanza in Whittier's hymn, entitled 'Our Master,' has the word 'Master' altered to 'Saviour' thereby obscuring the idea of the hymn, which is not the truth that Christ is our Saviour, but the truth that He is our Master.

Another verbal alteration that robs the hymn of its proper force:

'*When* the weary seeking rest,
  To Thy goodness flee;
When the heavy-laden cast
  All their load on Thee;'

and so on. The closing couplet in the same book is:

> 'Hear *Thou* in love, O Lord, the cry,
> In heaven Thy dwelling-place on high.'

The hymn was written, 'Hear *then*.' You see, the natural connection between 'when' and 'then' is quite lost. Why was the alteration made? Surely it might have been thought that its author, so accomplished a writer as Horatius Bonar, knew what he was about in writing 'then,' not 'Thou!'

In the 'Church Hymnary' and the 'Church Psalter' you will find that nearly every hymn has a modern and generally exceedingly feeble doxology tagged on to it.

The compiler evidently thought no hymn could be complete without a clear statement of the doctrine of the Trinity. Just fancy adding to Watts'

> 'There is a land of pure delight'

the utterly irrelevant lines:

> 'Lord Jesus, reign in us, we pray,
> And make us Thine alone,
> Who with the Father art
> And Holy Spirit one.'

My advice is, whenever you see a doxology to a hymn, to suspect its authenticity. Your suspicion will be justified ninety-nine times out of a hundred.

But the worst of all is the additional stanza you see, in some Church hymnals, to Newman's incomparable

> 'Lead, kindly Light,'

and this is the work of a dignitary of the Church of England. Bishop Bickersteth had the audacity to think that he could improve that hymn, and he added the following stanza:

> 'Meanwhile, along the narrow rugged path
>   Thyself hast trod,
> Lead, Saviour, lead me home in childlike faith,
>   Home to my God;
> To rest for ever after earthly strife
>   In the calm light of everlasting life.'

Now recall the construction of the hymn. Its opening thought is

> 'The night is dark, and I am far from home';

its closing one

> 'The night is gone,
>   And with the morn,' etc.—

beautifully complete as it stands: the prayer for leading answered, the longed-for home with its loved ones gained. What an anti-climax, then, to go back upon a 'Meanwhile!'

I hardly know which deserves the greater condemnation, the impertinence of attempting thus to gild refined gold, or the poverty of the language in which the attempt is made!*

I hold that a hymn is sacred in a double sense: it deals with sacred subjects, and should be held sacred as to its composition and sense. To me it appears as unwarrantable to add to a writer's hymns as it would be for a biographer, in editing a man's letters, to add to one of them a postscript of his own composition and to pass it off as original.

No words can be too strong to use in condemnation of such literary forgery; and the fact that it is

* This verse was subsequently withdrawn.

often committed in order to give a theological meaning not held by the author makes the act still more detestable. I can see no distinction in point of morality between this act and that of adding a codicil to another man's will.

I cannot bring my paper to a conclusion better than by quoting some sentences from a book called 'The Hymn Lover,' by Rev. W. G. Horder, which I cordially commend to any of you who may desire to follow this subject more closely. I desire to read this extract because it expresses in language better than I can find two beliefs I strongly hold: one, that there is no stronger evidence of the real unity of Christian men and women than is supplied by Christian hymns; and that the Golden Age of poetic hymns is not to be found in the past, but has only recently dawned, and has yet to grow to its fullest development:

'In many a case hymns are sung in assemblies in whose worship their authors would scarcely care to join, and whose doctrines they heartily condemn.

'The words of dean and bishop and cardinal are used in lowly conventicles where their stately canonicals would seem quite out of place; whilst, on the other hand, the hymns of many an unadorned layman belonging to the simpler Free Churches are sung by white-robed choristers and priests under the fluted roofs of venerable cathedrals.

'Thus one touch of (what is better than nature) grace makes the whole Church kin.

'Thus the hymns of the Presbyterian Bonar and the Independent Watts have passed into use, and are sung as parts of a richly ornate service; whilst, on the other hand, hymns by Cardinal Newman,

Hymns and their Writers

Bishop Christopher Wordsworth and Father Caswall have found their way into the simple services of village chapels. There is no bond of union stronger or more spiritual than that furnished by hymns which have sprung out of hearts kindled to lyric expression by the vision of Christ and His peerless work on behalf of men. Thus Christian feeling is proved to be mightier and more important in securing unity than the particular formulas which the minds of men have fashioned for its expression.

'For nowhere is the real unity underlying all diversity of the Church more clearly revealed than in the hymnody of these modern days.

'There are no helpers in the great work of quickening and deepening religious life whose aid is more precious than those whose love reaches its noblest expression in sacred song.

'Of late years the Church has been blessed with a large number of such helpers. Perhaps in no age has the number been so large, or the quality of the songs they have given us so high.

'From all quarters such songs have come: from laymen like George Rawson and Chatterton Dix, from the clergy of every rank, from the humble curate or country pastor to the right reverend bishop and the princely cardinal—nay, even* woman has had no mean place in this high work, for in many a church where women's voices may not be heard in speech they are heard in holy song (as in the hymns by Miss Havergal and Miss Elliott in "Hymns Ancient and Modern").

'Thus the lyric fervour sets at naught all ecclesiastical restrictions, all doctrinal exclusiveness. Thus

* Why 'even'?

may we catch gleams of the time when the whole Christian company shall be gathered, if not into one *fold*, yet into one *flock*, under the great shepherd, Christ. For of that time, so greatly desired, and often sought in such foolish ways, the truest heralds are the hymnists whose hearts are touched by the spirit of Christ.'

Printed by Libri Plureos GmbH in Hamburg, Germany